*Quick & Easy*

# Greeting Cards

*Quick & Easy*

# Greeting Cards

**15** step-by-step projects—simple to make, stunning results

CHERYL OWEN

CREATIVE
ARTS & CRAFTS™

An imprint of **CREATIVE HOMEOWNER**, Upper Saddle River, NJ

First published in the United States and Canada in 2004 by

# CRE A TIVE
## ARTS & CRAFTS™

An imprint of Creative Homeowner®
Upper Saddle River, NJ
Creative Homeowner® is a registered trademark of Federal Marketing Corp.

Current printing (last digit) 10 9 8 7 6 5 4 3 2 1
Library of Congress card number: 2004101635
ISBN: 1-58011-210-2

Senior Editor: Clare Hubbard
Production: Hazel Kirkman
Design: AG&G Books, Glyn Bridgewater
Photographer: Shona Wood
Templates: Steve Dew
Editorial Direction: Rosemary Wilkinson

Printed and bound in Malaysia

**Disclaimer**
The author and publishers have made every effort to ensure that all
instructions given in this book are safe and accurate, but they cannot accept
liability for any resulting injuries or loss or damage to either property or
person, whether direct or consequential and howsoever arising.

## CREATIVE HOMEOWNER
A division of Federal Marketing Corp.
24 Park Way
Upper Saddle River, NJ 07458
www.creativehomeowner.com

# Contents

 Projects

# Introduction

Giving a handcrafted greeting card shows the recipient just how much you care, and this book presents masses of innovative ideas for all sorts of special occasions. The most popular card-making techniques are explored in the projects, and they provide a great opportunity to try out new materials. Making the cards does not require much time and only the most basic tools.

There are projects for the beginner and the experienced card maker, and with so many special days to mark throughout the year, you'll never run out of reasons to be creative. It is surprising how quickly many of the cards can be made; which is great for when you want to produce multiples—for invitations or holiday cards, for example. On the other hand, a red letter day can be highlighted with a one-of-a-kind creation to be treasured. For an extra personal touch, there are instructions to show how your cards can be delivered in beautifully handcrafted envelopes.

Each project is accompanied by concise instructions and step-by-step photographs. Easy-to-use templates that will ensure a professional finish can be found on pages 74–77. Once you have mastered techniques that are new to you, start to be inventive and have fun creating your own wonderful designs.

#  Tools

For safety and best results, work in a well-lit area, on a clean, flat surface. Keep all of your tools away from children and pets.

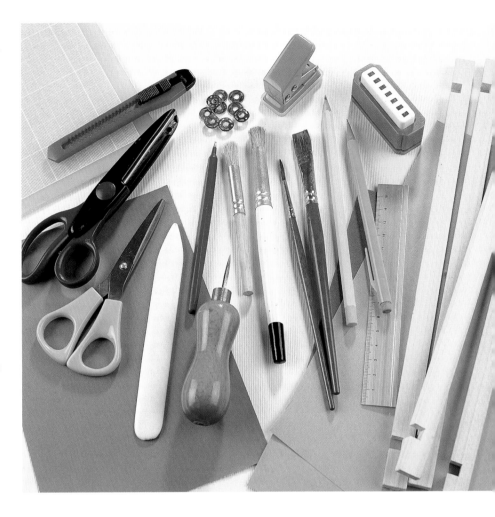

## Drawing

An HB pencil is the most useful for drawing. A softer pencil, such as a 2B, is recommended for transferring images. For accuracy, keep pencils sharpened to a point or use a lead-refill pencil. Use a ruler and T-square to draw squares and rectangles accurately.

## Cutting

A craft knife is indispensible for cutting straight lines. Craft knives are better than scissors for cutting cards because the paper can be kept flat. Work on a self-healing cutting mat when using a craft knife, cutting straight edges against a metal ruler. Change the blades often; a blunt blade will tear the surface of paper and cardstock. Always use caution when handling the blades. A craft knife can also be used to score card so that it folds neatly. However, a bone folder, which is a traditional bookbinding tool, is best for scoring, and worth buying if you intend to make a lot of greeting cards. It will also be useful for other paper crafts.

Choose scissors that are comfortable to handle; a sharp pair of general scissors are the most versatile. Small, intricate shapes can be cut with embroidery scissors. Pinking shears and fancy-edge scissors cut with a shaped edge can give a decorative touch to projects.

Paper punches come in all sorts of shapes and can be used to punch decorative holes in paper.

Pierce small holes with a pin or use an awl on a cutting mat for larger holes. A hole punch makes a neat hole quickly. Use wire cutters or an old pair of scissors to cut wire.

## Painting

A few good quality artist's paintbrushes such as a round brush, a flat brush, and a couple of stencil brushes are the most versatile for painting greeting cards. Expand the range if you intend to paint a lot of cards. Always clean brushes immediately after use.

Stretch silk if painting on a silk frame or improvise with an embroidery frame. Attach the silk to the frame with three-prong silk pins because they will not mark the silk.

### Safety

*When using any tools or materials, always follow the manufacturer's instructions carefully.*

# Materials

## Paper and cardstock

There is a superb choice of paper and cardstock that is available in art-supply, craft, and speciality paper stores today. Look for handmade papers incorporating petals, leaves, seeds, or metallic fragments, embossed with patterns and textured with fibers. Although handmade papers are often expensive, a single sheet will transform a greeting card. Translucent papers will subtly display the colors underneath them. There are also decorative papers that have glamorous surface embellishments such as embroidery or glitter. Create your own by stitching on paper with shiny thread or applying glitter with relief pens. High-quality stationers sell single sheets of writing paper in lots of colors. This is often an economic way of buying a small amount of paper with envelopes to match.

Cardstock comes in lots of different finishes, such as metallic and pearlized. Cut stencils from stencil sheets that have a waxed surface, which prevents paint from seeping. Corrugated cardstock is inexpensive and comes in a range of colors to match a project.

## Mixed media

Decorate your greeting cards with various craft materials. Emboss fine metal with simple images. Wire is available in different thicknesses and lovely colors from jewelry-making and craft suppliers. Use a pair of jewelry pliers to manipulate the wire. There is a wide range of rubber stamps available and inkpads in lots of shades; they offer a fast way to achieve a professional finish.

## Adhesives

Read the manufacturer's instructions and test adhesives on scrap paper before use. White glue is a very versatile, non-toxic adhesive. It will adhere paper, fabric, and wood. A glue-stick is good for use on paper. All-purpose household glue is surprisingly strong and will adhere many materials. It is best for gluing small areas, as it does not spread evenly over a large surface. Spread glue with a plastic glue spreader. Alternatively, improvise and spread glue with a scrap of cardstock. Use spray adhesive to bond layers of paper and cardstock. Double-sided tape is a clean, neat way to join paper and cardstock. Use adhesive foam to apply motifs so that they sit upright. Use low-tack masking tape to hold templates temporarily, but check first to see if it will tear or mark the work.

## Painting

Always use the correct paint for the job. Test paints on scrap paper and cardstock first. Some paints will warp them. Acrylic paints can be mixed easily and will dry quickly.

Glass paints give a luxurious, transparent color on acetate. They come in a large range of colors and can be mixed. Apply glass outliner to acetate first to create different areas. Then flood the areas with the glass paints. Use silk paints on silk material. These are water-based paints that are applied in a similar way to glass paints. Use silk outliner (gutta) to draw the shapes on stretched silk. Then fill in the outlined shapes with paint.

Relief paints in pearlized and glitter finishes are simple and fun to use. Designs painted with masking fluid can be painted over, then rubbed to reveal the paper underneath.

## Decoration

It is often the small embellishments that make a greeting card special. For glamour add beads, sequins, and cabochon jewelry stones. Finish with silky cords and tassels.

Unexpected everyday items can also be incorporated; save foil candy wrappers, buttons, and scraps of ribbon and lace for use on your cards. Colorful pieces of wallpaper and wrapping paper are ideal for making greeting cards.

Nature also provides a host of decorations. Press flowers and leaves from the backyard and collect tiny shells, pebbles, and feathers when you're out walking.

If you will be adding three-dimensional elements, consider how you will pack the card, especially if it is to be mailed. Use a padded envelope or hand-deliver a card in a box. Decorate envelopes that will be delivered by hand to coordinate with the greeting card.

*Materials are shown on page 10.*

*Materials. See page 9 for descriptions.*

# Techniques

The same basic techniques occur throughout the projects. Always read the instructions for a project before embarking upon it and try out new techniques on scrap paper first.

## Using templates

Trace the image onto tracing paper, drawing straight lines against a ruler. Turn the tracing over and re-draw it on the wrong side with a soft pencil. Use masking tape to hold the tracing right side up on your chosen paper or cardstock. Re-draw the design to transfer it using a sharp HB pencil. If you wish to use the template more than once or twice, transfer it onto thin cardstock to cut out and draw around.

## Enlarging and reducing templates on a photocopier

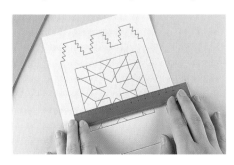

For speed and accuracy, use a photocopier to enlarge or reduce a motif. You will need to calculate your enlargement percentage. First decide what width you want the final image to be. Then measure the width of the original motif that you want to photocopy. Divide the first measurement by the second one. Then multiply the answer by 100 to find the percentage by which you need to enlarge the motif. For example, say a 4-inch motif needs to be enlarged to 6 inches. Using the calculation, you can work out that 6 divided by 4 and then multliplied by 100 equals an increase of 150 percent. Remember that an enlargement must always be more than 100 percent and a reduction must be less than 100 percent.

## Enlarging and reducing templates on a grid

To enlarge or reduce a motif by hand

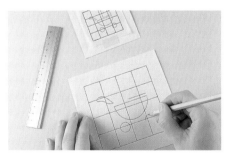

on a grid, tape a piece of tracing paper over the original design. Draw a square or rectangle to enclose the image. Then divide it up with a row of equally spaced vertical and horizontal lines. The spacing will depend upon the size and intricacy of the design. Complex designs should

have lines that are about ³/₈ inch apart; simpler ones will have lines that are about 1 inch apart.

Draw a square or rectangle of the required finished size to the same proportions as the square or rectangle on the tracing paper. Divide it into the same number of vertical and horizontal lines. Re-draw the image working on one square or rectangle at a time. Then view the design as a whole and re-draw any areas that do not seem to flow well.

## Using a craft knife

Cut straight edges on paper with a craft knife and a metal ruler. Work on a cutting mat. When cutting cardstock, do not press too hard or attempt to cut through it on the first approach. It is easier to cut deeper gradually.

## Scoring

It is easier to fold cardstock neatly if a fold line has been scored first. A bone folder, (a traditional book-binder's tool), is recommended for scoring; score with the pointed end against a ruler. Alternatively, lightly score with a craft knife taking care not to cut through the paper.

## Folding

A bone folder is useful for folding paper and cardstock. Press the flat of the bone folder on the fold and run it smoothly along its length. If you do not have a bone folder, press your thumb along the fold to flatten it.

## Using spray adhesive

Always use spray adhesive in a well-ventilated room and protect the surrounding area with newspaper. If adhering large pieces, smooth them out from the center for an even finish.

## Strengthening paper

Fine paper can be used for making greeting cards. To strengthen the paper, cut it approximately 1/2 inch

larger than the finished size. Spray-mount the paper to cardstock, smoothing it outwards from the center. Cut it to the required size.

## Creating a deckle edge

**1** Place a ruler on the paper where you wish to tear it. Dip an artist's paintbrush in water and run it along the ruler's edge to soften the paper or cardstock. If the cardstock is very thick, you may need to repeat the process on the other side.

**2** Holding the ruler firmly in position, tear the paper against it.

## Making an insert

An insert gives a formal touch. It is useful to add a light-colored insert if the inside of the greeting card is dark color and difficult to read. Open the card out flat. Cut the insert paper 1/4 inch smaller than the cardstock on all sides. Fold the insert in half. Run a line of glue stick close to the fold of the insert. Stick it inside the back of the greeting card, matching the folds.

## Making a basic envelope

**1** To make a template, measure the card front and draw it on scrap paper adding 1/4 inch to each edge. Draw the flap on the upper edge half the width of the front. Draw the back at the lower edge, 1 1/2 inches less than the width of the front. Draw a 1-inch-wide tab each side of the front. Draw a curve at each corner; a coin or button is a useful template for the curves.

**2** Cut out the template and draw around it on paper or thin cardstock. Score along the edges of the front with a bone folder or lightly with a craft knife. Fold along the lines, folding the tabs under the back.

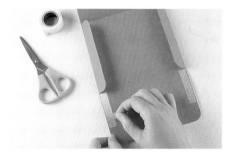

**3** Open out the back again. Apply $^1/_2$-inch-wide double-sided tape along the side edges of the inner back, starting 1 inch below the upper edge. Peel off the backing tapes and stick the back over the tabs. Tuck the flap inside the back or seal it with double-sided tape.

## Making a lined envelope
Choose thin paper or gift wrapping for the lining so the envelope folds neatly and is not too bulky and untidy.

Follow step 1 for, "Making a basic envelope," on the previous page. Cut the front and flap shape from the lining paper, trimming $^1/_4$ inch from the outer edges. Stick the lining to the inside of the envelope, $^1/_4$ inch inside the edges, with spray adhesive. Continue making up the envelope following the basic envelope steps 2 and 3.

## Making a padded envelope
Present delicate greeting cards in a padded envelope for protection.

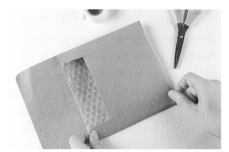

Measure the card front and draw it on scrap paper adding $^3/_8$ inch to each edge. Draw up the envelope referring to the "Making a basic envelope". Cut out the envelope. Cut the front and back shape from bubble wrap and stick it to the inside of the envelope using spray adhesive, with the smooth side of the bubble wrap uppermost. Apply $^1/_2$-inch-wide double-sided tape along the side edges of the tabs on the inside, starting $2^1/_4$ inches below the upper edge. Fold the back over the front. Peel off the backing tapes and stick the tabs over the back. Seal the flap over the back with double-sided tape.

## Making a box envelope
Present a hand-delivered greeting card in a custom-made box. For protection, line the box and lid with bubble wrap, fill the box with shredded tissue, or wrap the card in tissue paper.
**1** Measure the card front and draw it on scrap paper, adding $^1/_4$ inch to each edge. This will be the base. Measure the depth of the card (take into account items that stand away). Draw a side to the base along each edge that is the depth of the

card plus $^1/_4$ inch. Add a $^3/_4$-inch-wide tab to both ends of two opposite box sides and draw a slanted end to the tabs.

**2** Cut out the template and use it to cut a box from cardstock. Score along the lines with a bone folder or a craft knife. Fold the side edges upward. Stick the tabs under the opposite ends of the sides with double-sided tape. Make a lid in the same way as the box but adding $^1/_{10}$ inch to each edge of the base.

## Adapting craft techniques
If you have a favorite craft, adapt it for making greeting cards less time-consuming to make. Embroider simple motifs for example, or paint a series of characters that can be cut out and used separately. By experimenting you will find ways to simplify the technique without losing its appeal.

# 3-D birdhouse

Send a charming birdhouse to the proud owner of a new home. The three-dimensional house folds flat to fit into an envelope. A real twig, attached to the front, is a delightful finishing touch. The roof is made of vibrant corrugated cardstock and the house is constructed from ridged cardstock. Write your message on the underside of the roof.

Ordinary corrugated paper can be used for the roof. Simply paint it a bright color.

## You will need

### Materials
- Tracing paper
- Masking tape
- An 8½ x 11-in. sheet of white ridged cardstock
- Double-sided tape
- A 5 x 8-in. sheet of red or blue corrugated cardstock
- Small twig
- All-purpose household glue

### Tools
- Soft pencil
- Cutting mat
- Craft knife
- Bone folder (optional)
- Metal ruler
- Scissors

**1** Trace the birdhouse template on page 74 onto tracing paper with a soft pencil. Turn the tracing over and draw the birdhouse. Tape the tracing right side up on white ridged paper. Re-draw the birdhouse to transfer the image. Remove the tracing. Cut out the house and the hole with a craft knife, on a cutting mat.

**2** Score the birdhouse along the broken lines using a bone folder or craft knife. Apply double-sided tape to the tabs on the right side. Fold the birdhouse along the scored lines with the inner sides facing to form the birdhouse shape.

★☆☆ **Skill level**    🕐 **2 hours**    **Techniques:** *Using templates p. 11, Using a craft knife p. 11, Scoring p. 11, Folding p.12*

**3** Peel the backing tape off the house tab. Stick the tab under the opposite end of the birdhouse.

**4** Trace the roof template on page 74 onto tracing paper with a soft pencil. Turn the paper over and re-draw the roof. Transfer the roof template to red or blue corrugated cardstock with the corrugations parallel with the short edges. Draw the tab position on the inside. Fold the roof in half, then open it out flat.

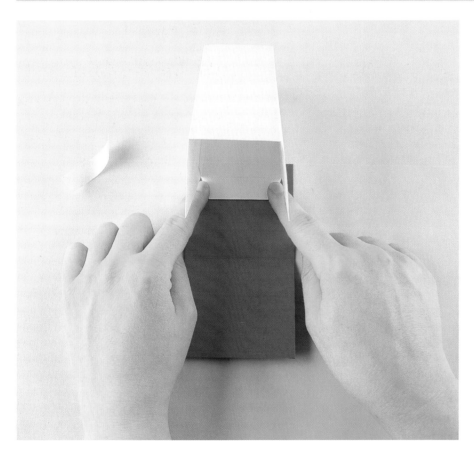

**5** Peel the backing tape off the roof tab on the house. With the roof inside facing up, stick the house roof tab onto the tab position on the inside of the roof. Fold the other end of the roof over the top of the birdhouse.

**6** To add a perch, glue a small twig to the front of the bird house.

## Helpful hint

When mailing this card, slip a piece of bubble-wrap into the envelope to protect the twig perch from damage.

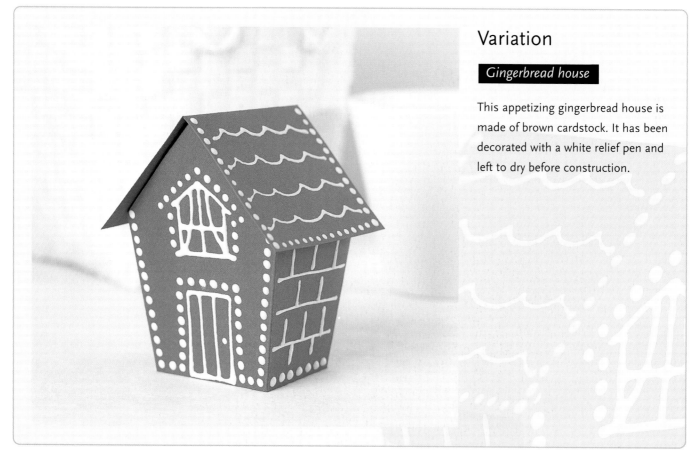

## Variation

**Gingerbread house**

This appetizing gingerbread house is made of brown cardstock. It has been decorated with a white relief pen and left to dry before construction.

# Anniversary image transfer

**The treasured family photograph on this glamorous greeting card has been photocopied then embellished with glitter and cabochon jewelry stones. A silk border, flamboyant organza ribbon, and beads add to its opulence. Include an insert to give the greeting extra importance.**

Do not use heirloom photographs to make greeting card. Photocopy your favorites so the originals can be kept safe and intact.

## You will need

### Materials

- Postcard-size photo
- Glitter relief paints
- Medium-weight pink silk ($3/4$ in. larger than photo)
- Spray adhesive
- An 11 x 17-in. sheet of white cardstock
- Selection of cabochon jewelry stones
- All-purpose household glue
- An 11 x 17-in. sheet of antique white paper
- Glue stick
- 1 yard of $1/2$-in. wide pink organza ribbon
- 8 small crystal beads with large holes
- 2 large pink beads with large holes

### Tools

- Craft knife
- Metal ruler
- Cutting mat
- Fabric scissors
- Bone folder (optional)
- Tweezers (optional)
- Large-eye needle

**1** Photocopy the image and cut it out, trimming it to a different size if you wish. Highlight details on the photo using glitter relief paints.

**2** Cut a rectangle of pink silk that is $3/4$ inch larger on all sides than the copied image. Affix the image to the silk with spray adhesive.

★★☆ **Skill level**    🕐 **2 hours**    **Techniques:** *Scoring p. 11, Folding p. 12, Using spray adhesive p. 12, Making an insert p. 12*

3 Cut an 8 x 13-inch rectangle of white cardstock. Score it across the center, parallel with the short edges. Fold the card in half along the scored line. Affix the image to the front with spray adhesive. Glue a cabochon jewelry stone at each corner with all-purpose household glue. Use tweezers to position the stones if it is easier to work this way.

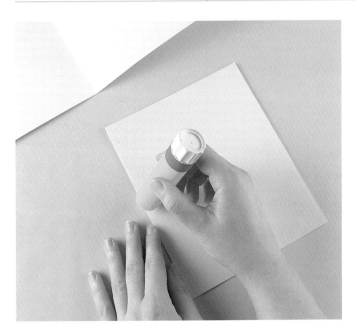

4 Cut a 7³/₄ x 12³/₄-inch rectangle of antique white paper to use as an insert. Fold the insert in half, parallel with the short edges. Run a line of glue stick close to the fold then mount the insert inside the back of the greeting card, matching the folds.

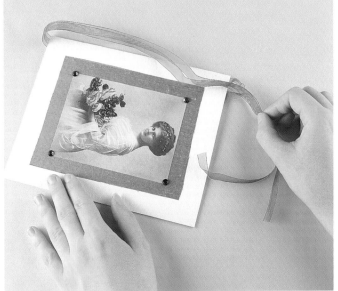

5 Fold the ribbon in half; and slip it inside the card between the pages of the insert with the fold at the top. Close the card; and bring the ends of the ribbon up over the front of the card and through the loop at the top.

**6** Thread a needle on one ribbon end; slip three crystal beads, one pink bead, and another crystal bead on the ribbon. Knot the ribbon under the beads. Repeat on the other end. Carefully cut off the excess ribbon.

## Helpful hint
If you do not have a needle with an eye that is large enough for the ribbon, bend fine wire in half and slip the ribbon through the fold and use the wire as a needle. Alternatively, you could use a bodkin.

## Variation

**White silk**

This elegant photocopied image has been applied to white silk with a frayed edge. A few simple embroidery stitches worked in gold thread add understated decoration.

# Beaded-heart accordian

An accordian greeting card provides a lot of space to write long messages or insert photographs. Its pages open in folds and both sides can contain writing. The cover is decorated with a bold heart that is worked from beaded wire.

The heart is an ideal motif for a Valentine card and the pages allow a lengthy, heartfelt message to be written.

## You will need

### aMaterials

- 24-gauge wire
- Assorted pink beads
- An $8^{1}/_{2}$ x 11-in. sheet of thick white card
- An 11 x 17-in. sheet of purple paper
- White glue
- Matching thread
- An 17 x 22-in. sheet of thick red paper

### Tools

- Wire cutters or an old pair of scissors
- Jeweler's pliers
- Craft knife
- Metal ruler
- Cutting mat
- Glue spreader
- Needle
- Scissors
- Bone folder (optional)

**1** Snip an $11^{1}/_{2}$-inch length of wire. Bend an inch of the wire at one end to stop the beads from slipping off the end. Thread assorted pink beads onto the wire stopping 1 inch from the other end.

## Helpful hint
Always snip wire with wire cutters or an old pair of scissors because the wire will blunt shears.

★★☆ **Skill level**    🕐 **3 hours**    **Techniques:** *Using a craft knife p.11, Scoring p.11, Folding p.12*

**2**  Link the ends of the wire together with a pair of jeweler's pliers, forming a ring. Bend the ring into a heart shape, making sure the join forms the bottom point. Snip off the excess wire.

**3**  Working on a cutting mat, use a craft knife to cut two 4½-inch squares of thick white cardstock and two 6-inch squares of purple paper for the front and back of the card. Center the card squares on the reverse side of the papers. Glue the corners, then the edges of the paper over the card.

**4**  Place the heart on the front. Pierce two holes with the needle, one on either side of the top point of the heart. Thread the needle; push it up through one hole from the reverse side and down through the other hole capturing the heart against the front. Tie the thread ends securely on the reverse side.

**5**  Cut a 21¼-inch-long strip of 4½-inch-wide red paper for the pages. Score the pages with a bone folder or lightly with a craft knife. Make accordian folds that are 4¼-inches wide.

**6** Spread glue evenly on the back page with a glue spreader. Mount the pages in the center of the reverse side of the back cover. Spread glue on the front page, and press the front cover on top, lining it up with the back cover.

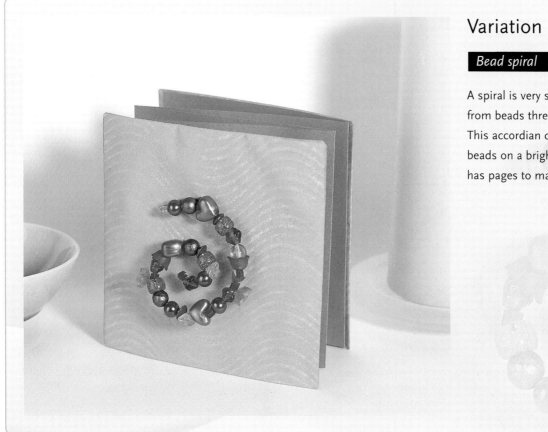

## Variation

**Bead spiral**

A spiral is very simple to model from beads threaded onto wire. This accordian card with vibrant blue beads on a bright green background has pages to match the beads.

# Embossed metal fern

Subtle effects are achieved by embossing designs on metal flashing, which is available in sheet form from craft stores. This handsome fern is set off by the metal stud fastening. An insert of matching translucent paper lends a formal tone to this greeting card.

Metal studs are easy to apply. They come in lots of different shapes and are available from craft stores.

## You will need

### Materials
- Tracing paper
- An 8½ x 11-in. sheet of metal flashing
- Masking tape
- Paper towel
- An 11 x 17-in. sheet of bright green card
- 3 round metal studs
- An 11 x 17-in. sheet of bright green translucent paper
- All-purpose household glue

### Tools
- Pen
- Metal cutters or an old pair of scissors
- Scissors
- Ballpoint pen
- Cutting mat
- Craft knife
- Metal ruler
- Bone folder (optional)
- Awl

**1** Trace the fern template on page 75 onto tracing paper with a pen. With a pair of metal cutters or an old pair of scissors, cut a 5¼ x 8-inch rectangle of metal flashing. Tape the tracing right side up on top with masking tape.

**2** Place the metal and tracing on two sheets of paper towel. To emboss the design, trace the ferns with a ballpoint pen. Remove the tracing.

★★☆ **Skill level**    🕐 **2 hours**    **Techniques:** *Using templates p.11, Using a craft knife p.11, Scoring, p.11, Using spray adhesive p. 12*

**3** Working on a cutting mat, use a craft knife to cut two 7³/₄ x 9¹/₄-inch rectangles of bright green cardstock for the front and back. Using a bone folder or craft knife, score the front of the paper, beginning 1¹/₄-inches in from the left edge to create a hinge.

## Helpful hint
If you have one, use a special embossing tool on the metal, rather than a ballpoint pen.

**4** Place a stud in the center of the hinge. Press the stud to make indentations with the prongs. Position the remaining studs ³/₄ inch from the upper and lower edges. Indent the hinge with the prongs to mark the positions of the studs.

**5** Working on a cutting mat, use a craft knife to cut two 7¹/₂ x 9-inch rectangles of green translucent paper for the inserts. Place the back of the cardstock on the cutting mat, position the inserts on top with the left edges even and the card extending ¹/₈ inch above and below the inserts. Place the front on top.

**6** Use an awl to enlarge the prong holes, pierce them through to the back page.

**7** Starting at the center, insert the prongs of a stud through the holes and close them over the back card to secure all the layers together. Fix the other studs in the same way. Glue the fern to the front.

# Resist-painted Easter egg

**Welcome springtime with a colorful, jaunty Easter egg. The vibrant colors on this greeting card are painted over patterns created with masking fluid that is rubbed away, when the paint has dried, to reveal the paper underneath.**

To make the motifs stand away from the card, fix them in place with pieces of adhesive foam.

## You will need

### Materials

- An 11 x 17 in. sheet of watercolor paper
- Masking fluid
- Tracing paper
- Masking tape
- Scrap paper
- Pink, lilac, light blue, and yellow acrylic paints
- Adhesive foam

### Tools

- Craft knife
- Metal ruler
- Cutting mat
- Artist's paintbrush
- Soft pencil
- Scissors
- Flat ³/₄-in. paintbrush
- Bone folder (optional)
- Fancy-edged scissors

**1** Cut a 7 x 10-inch rectangle of watercolor paper. With an artist's paintbrush, randomly apply spots of masking fluid to the paper, and then leave it to dry.

**2** With a soft pencil, draw a 1¹/₄ x 4¹/₄-inch strip for the borders on watercolor paper. Trace the egg on page 75 onto tracing paper with a soft pencil. Tape the tracing face down on the watercolor paper with masking tape. Re-draw the egg to transfer it, then remove the tracing paper.

★★☆ **Skill level**     🕐 **3 hours**     **Techniques:** *Using templates p.11, Using a craft knife p. 11, Scoring p.11, Folding p.12*

**3** Using an artist's paintbrush, paint stripes on the strip and simple patterns on the egg with masking fluid. Leave it to dry.

**4** Working on a sheet of scrap paper, use a flat brush to paint the rectangle of watercolor paper yellow. (This is the card base.) Thin the paint with water so that brush strokes are visible in places. An even coverage is not necessary.

## Helpful hint
When painting the watercolor paper, work quickly to give a free, loose effect.

**5** Paint the strip pink and the egg with lilac, light blue, and yellow. As before, thin the paints with water. When the paint has dried, gently rub off the masking fluid with your finger. Using a bone folder or craft knife, score across the center of the card base, parallel with the short edges. Fold the card along the scored line.

## Helpful hint

If you do not have a pair of fancy edged scissors, use pinking shears instead. Alternatively, cut a wavy edge with straight scissors.

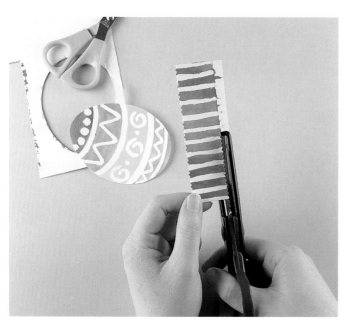

**6** Working on a cutting mat, cut across the ends of the pink and white strip. Cut out the egg with a craft knife. Cut just inside the long edges of the strip with a pair of fancy-edged scissors. Then cut the strip in half lengthwise.

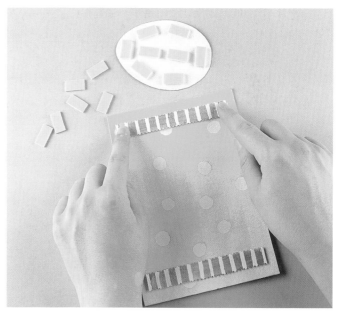

**7** Stick pieces of adhesive foam to the reverse side of the strips. Apply a double-thick layer of the foam to the egg. Peel off the backing tapes. Center the strips ½-inch in from the short edges of the card base. Mount the egg in the center.

# Embossed baby booties

Here is a charming greeting card to welcome a new baby. The baby buggy and booties are embossed through a stencil to subtly create the motifs that are framed with fun foam. Bands of contrasting papers are embellished with cutouts made with a paper punch.

Colored writing paper is ideal to use for embossing. Choose 67-pound weight paper.

## You will need

### Materials
- Tracing paper
- Stencil board
- Masking tape
- A 5 x 8-in. sheet of light blue or pink writing paper
- A 5 x 8-in. piece of yellow fun foam
- Spray adhesive
- A 5 x 8-in. sheet of green paper
- A 8½ x 11-in. sheet of purple cardstock

### Tools
- Soft pencil
- Scissors
- Craft knife
- Metal ruler
- Cutting mat
- Ball embossing tool
- "Row of rectangles" paper punch
- Bone folder (optional)

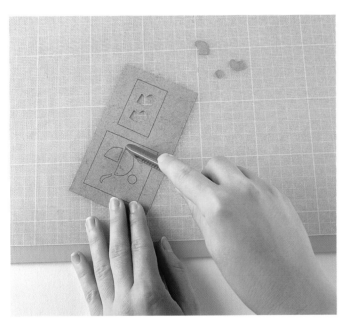

**1** Trace the templates on page 74 onto tracing paper with a soft pencil. Turn the tracing over and re-draw the motifs on the reverse. Tape the tracing paper right side up on stencil board with masking tape. Transfer the motifs. Remove the tracing. Working on a cutting mat, cut out the motifs with a craft knife.

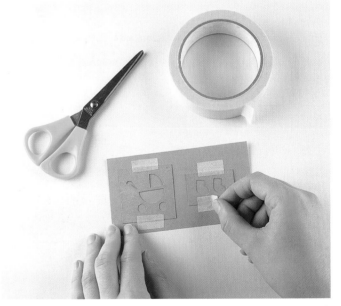

**2** Tape the stencil right side up on the right side of light blue or pink writing paper with masking tape. Turn the paper over.

★★☆ **Skill level**    ⏱ **3 hours**    **Techniques:** *Using templates p. 11, Using a craft knife p. 11, Using spray adhesive p. 12*

**3** Rub through the stencil with a ball embossing tool. The design will be embossed on the right side of the paper. Draw around the outer edge of the stencils. Remove the stencil. Cut along the drawn outer edges.

## Helpful hint
Instead of an embossing tool, a knitting needle or the rounded handle end of an artist's paint-brush can be used to emboss the motifs.

**4** Working on a cutting mat, use a craft knife to cut a 2½-inch square and a 1½ x 2¼-inch rectangle from fine yellow foam. Center the embossed motifs on the foam with spray adhesive.

**5** Cut a 2¾ x 3½-inch and a 2½ x 3-inch rectangle of green paper. Punch a centered row of rectangles along one short edge of each green rectangle with a paper punch. Press hard so that the cuts have neat edges.

**6** Cut a 6³/₄ x 9¹/₂-inch rectangle of purple cardstock. Using a bone folder or craft knife, score across the center, parallel with the short edges. Fold the card in half along the scored line. Arrange the green paper rectangles on the card front. Position the foam on top. Stick all the pieces in place with spray adhesive.

## Variation

**Fancy pram**

This three-dimensional greeting card has an embossed baby buggy that is bordered by two layers of colored fun foam, one of which has been cut with fancy-edged scissors.

# Christmas purse

These unique Christmas cards will add a surprise to the festive celebrations. The little bags of translucent paper contain a folded message and a scattering of Christmas sequins. Once the contents have been revealed, the purses can be hung on the Christmas tree.

These pretty containers are also ideal for wedding and Valentine celebrations. Simply add a suitable sequin motif, such as a heart.

## You will need

**Materials**

- A 5 x 8-in. sheet of colored translucent paper
- Double-sided tape
- Tracing paper
- Scrap of thin cardstock (optional)
- Gold-glitter relief-paint
- 12 in. of fine gold cord
- Festive sequin shapes
- All-purpose household glue
- A 5 x 8-in. sheet of gold paper

**Tools**

- Scissors
- Pencil
- Craft knife
- Metal ruler
- Cutting mat
- Bone folder (optional)
- Awl

**1** Cut a 3 x 7-inch rectangle of colored translucent paper. Score across the center, parallel with the short edges and fold the paper in half. Cut double-sided tape into two ¼-inch wide x 3¼-inch long strips and stick them along the long edges on one side. Fold down the other side to make the bag.

**2** Trace the purse template on page 75 onto tracing paper and cut it out. If you wish to make a number of purses, cut the purse from thin cardstock to make a durable template. Align the template and draw the scallops. Cut along the scallops.

★★☆ **Skill level**    🕐 **3 hours**    **Techniques:** *Using templates p. 11, Using a craft knife p. 11, Scoring p. 11, Folding p. 12*

**3** Starting ³/₄-inch below the upper edge, apply gold-glitter relief-paint down the side edges. Leave the glitter to dry.

## Helpful hint

Loose glitter can be used instead of glitter relief paint. Dot white glue on the bag, sprinkle with loose glitter, and shake off the excess.

**4** Working on a cutting mat, pierce a hole at the top corners of the bag with an awl. Thread the cord through the holes, and knot the ends on the front. Cut off the excess cord.

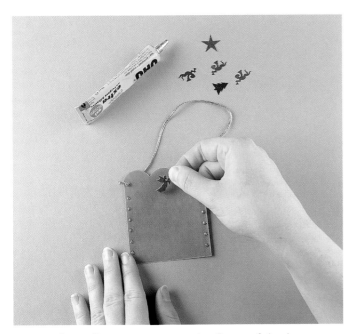

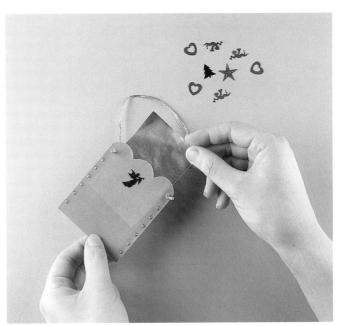

**5** Glue a festive sequin to the front of the bag. Make sure that you apply the glue sparingly, so it does not seep onto the paper. Alternatively, adhere the sequin with a piece of double-sided tape.

**6** Cut a 2 1/2 x 7-inch rectangle of gold paper. Write a message on the paper, and fold it in half, parallel with the short edges. Slip the message into the bag, folded edge first. Carefully pour some sequins inside the message.

## Variation

**Pink handbag**

This pretty pink paper purse is decorated with silver glitter and suspended on pink ribbon.

# Driftwood ship

Here is a romantic sailing ship made from various recycled materials. The ship sails on a painted sea; its hull is a piece of driftwood; and the sail is part of a map. With its traveling theme, this greeting card would make a delightful bon-voyage card.

The off-white background paper is subtly printed with white shells to echo the nautical theme.

## You will need

### Materials

- An 11 x 17-in. sheet of off-white patterned paper
- An 11 x 17-in. sheet of off-white card
- Spray adhesive
- Blue, aquamarine, and off-white acrylic paint
- Tracing paper
- Masking tape
- A 5 x 8 in. piece of old map
- 4³/₄-in. curved twig
- Scrap of fabric
- All-purpose household glue
- Piece of driftwood, approx. 2 x 4¹/₂ in.

### Tools

- Metal ruler
- Craft knife
- Cutting mat
- Bone folder (optional)
- Flat ³/₄-in. paintbrush
- Soft pencil
- Scissors
- Hole punch

**1** To strengthen the background paper, adhere a 9 x 14-inch rectangle of off-white patterned paper to off-white card with spray adhesive. Cut out a 8¹/₂ x 13¹/₄-inch rectangle. Score across the center, parallel with the short edges, using a bone folder or craft knife. Fold along the scored line.

**2** Mix together blue, aquamarine, and off-white acrylic paints. Pick up a little of the paint on a flat paintbrush. Paint across the lower 2¹/₄ inches of the front of the card. Do not coat the card evenly. Allow the paper to show through in places. Leave to dry.

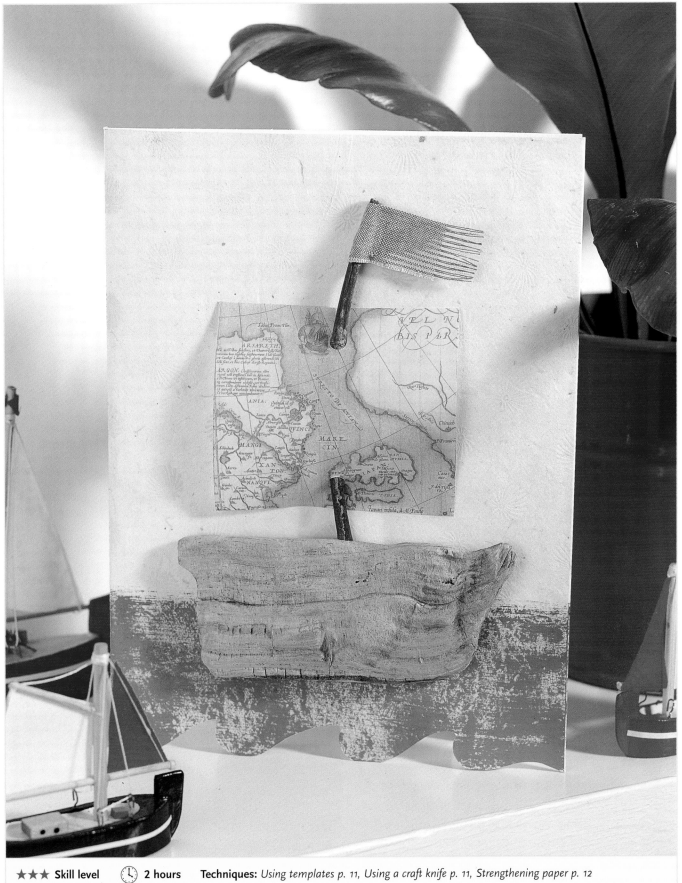

★★★ **Skill level** ⏱ **2 hours**     **Techniques:** *Using templates p. 11, Using a craft knife p. 11, Strengthening paper p. 12*

3 Trace the template on page 75 onto tracing paper with a soft pencil. Turn the tracing over and draw the waves on the reverse side. Tape the tracing to the lower edge of the front of the card with masking tape. Draw the waves on the lower edge to transfer them. Remove the tracing. Working on a cutting mat, cut out the waves through both the front and back of the card using a craft knife.

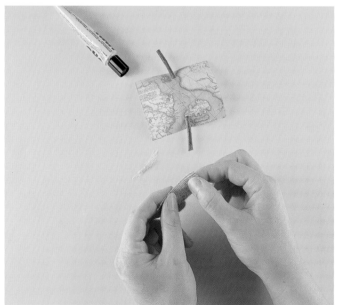

4 Cut an 3 x 3 1/4-inch rectangle from an old map for the sail. With a hole punch, make a hole in the center of each of the long edges. Insert the twig, which will be the mast, through the punched holes.

5 Cut a 3/4 x 2-inch rectangle from a scrap of fabric for the flag. Fray one short edge. Wrap the unfrayed edge of the flag around the top of the mast and glue it in place.

**6** Arrange the pieces on the front of the card. Glue the driftwood hull, the mast, and finally, the sail in position. Lay the card flat while the glue dries.

## Helpful hint
If you do not have a suitable piece of driftwood, cut a hull from balsa wood using a craft knife.

## Variation

### Little boat

This driftwood boat has two metal eyelets screwed into the top of its driftwood hull. A hole has been pierced in the center with an awl and a twig mast is inserted. Fine string is tied to the eyelets and bound around the top of the twig. A fabric flag tops the mast, and the boat is glued to blue cloud-effect paper that is applied to a turquoise blue card base.

# Pressed-flower trellis

Gather pretty flowers to make this beautiful greeting card, which is ideal for a nature lover. The trellis effect is made from pressed lavender sprigs and stems that are fastened with raffia. The trellis then frames a set of colorful pressed flowers. Applying the design to handmade paper that is embedded with petals emphasizes the floral theme.

Pressed leaves would make a great alternative to flowers. Choose foliage in rich fall shades for a birthday later in the year. Use stems with a small leaf at the tip for the uprights of the trellis.

## You will need

### Materials

* Fresh flowers, including lavender sprigs
* Blotting paper
* An 11 x 17-in. sheet of thick handmade paper embedded with petals
* White glue
* Raffia

### Tools

* Flower press (or heavy book)
* Metal ruler
* Fine artist's paintbrush
* Bone folder or craft knife
* Glue spreader
* Scissors
* Large-eyed needle
* Tweezers

**1** Pick flower heads no wider than 1¼-inches and lavender sprigs. Pick more than you need in case they break or the petals crease. Carefully place the flowers between layers of blotting paper and press them flat in a flower press for about one week. Gently peel back the papers to reveal the pressed flowers.

**2** To tear a deckle-effect edge, place a ruler on thick handmade paper. Moisten a fine artist's paintbrush and run it along the paper against the ruler to weaken the paper. Tear the paper against the ruler to make two 6-inch squares for the front and back of the card.

★★★ **Skill level**    🕐 **3 hours**    **Techniques:** *Scoring p. 11, Tearing a deckle edge p. 12*

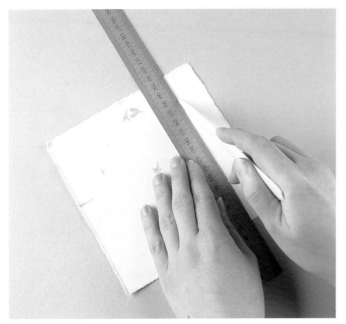

**3** On one of the squares, score a margin 1¼-inches in from the left-hand edge with a bone folder or craft knife to make a hinge. Bend the hinge forwards. This is the front of the card.

**4** Arrange three pressed lavender sprigs upright on the card front 1½-inches apart and ½-inch below the top edge. Glue the heads in place.

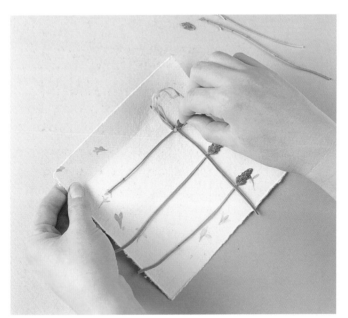

**5** Cut the heads off another three lavender sprigs. Lay one stem horizontally across the upright sprigs below the heads. Thread the needle with raffia, then bring it from the back to the right side and sew a cross over the sprigs at the two outer intersections to secure. Tie the raffia ends together on the underside.

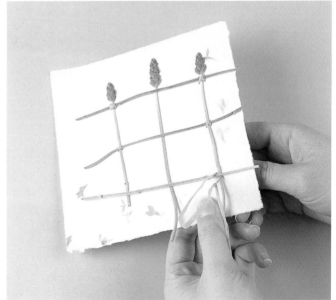

**6** Lay the remaining stems across the uprights 1½-inches apart forming a trellis and sew in place as before. Trim the sprigs to ½-inch beyond the trellis.

**7** Use a pair of tweezers to gently lift the flowers from the blotting paper. Use a glue spreader to spread white glue sparingly on the flower heads and stick a flower within each trellis square.

**8** Glue a pressed lavender sprig on the hinge. Place the card front onto the back. Sew the sprig in place through both card layers with raffia in a cross stitch at the top and bottom of the stem, tying the ends securely on the back. Cut off the excess raffia.

## Variation

**Bunch of flowers**

Bunch together a group of pressed lavender sprigs on the front of a folded rectangle of handmade paper embedded with petals and leaves. Stick the arrangement in place with white glue. Thread a large-eyed needle with fine silk ribbon and bind it a few times round the stems by sewing through the card. Tie the ribbon on the front of the card.

# Rubber-stamped Dutch scene

Creating designs with a rubber stamp is a great way to get professional results very quickly. This greeting card features a stamped picture of a tranquil Dutch scene embellished with scraps of lace, ribbon, and buttons. The back of the greeting card extends beyond the front opening edge and has a decorative border that is still visible when the recipient opens the card to read it.

*If you don't have a stamp with a windmill scene, you can substitute with another scene or motif.*

## You will need

### Materials

- Blue ink pad
- An 8½ x 11-in. sheet of white cardstock
- An 11 x 17-in. sheet of off-white ridged cardstock
- Spray adhesive
- Scraps of edging lace
- ½-in.-wide blue gingham ribbon
- Red stranded-cotton embroidery thread
- 4 red buttons
- All-purpose household glue

### Tools

- Windmill rubber stamp
- Craft knife
- Cutting mat
- Metal ruler
- Bone folder (optional)
- Needlework scissors
- Large crewel embroidery needle

**1** Gently press the rubber stamp onto the ink pad. Make sure to load the entire stamp with ink. Stamp the picture onto white cardstock and allow it to dry. Working on a cutting baord, use a craft knife to cut out the picture, leaving a ½-inch border on all sides. Measure the picture including the border.

**2** Cut a piece of cardstock that is the height of the picture plus 1¼ inches, and twice its width plus 3½ inches including the border. Along one long edge of the cardstock, measure the width of the picture plus 2½ inches. Score across the card at this point. Fold. Mount the picture to the front with spray adhesive.

★★★ **Skill level**    🕐 **2 hours**    **Techniques:** *Scoring p. 11, Using spray adhesive p. 12*

**3** Use spray adhesive to apply wide lace to the inside of the card along the extending right-hand edge. Adhere a length of gingham ribbon on top. Cut the ends of the lace and ribbon even with the card.

**4** Using spray adhesive, apply narrow lace along each side of the picture. Cut the ends of the lace even with the card using scissors.

**5** Thread a large crewel embroidery needle with six strands of red stranded-cotton embroidery thread. Sew a running stitch along the two narrow strips of edging lace, fastening the ends of the thread on the underside of the card. Cut off the excess thread.

**6** As a finishing touch, glue a red button to each corner of the picture using all-purpose household glue.

## Helpful hint
To emboss the stamped picture, sprinkle embossing powder on the design while the ink is still wet. Shake off the excess powder. Carefully fix the powder using a precision heat tool.

# Wire dragonfly

This elegant dragonfly is modeled from colored wire and its wings accentuated with translucent paper. Vibrant colored wires in various thicknesses are now available from craft stores and speciality suppliers. They bend easily and are ideal for craft work. The dragonfly is applied to a background of white paper embedded with colorful fibers, then framed with a bold, metallic turquoise card.

Modeling the dragonfly with wire allows the design to be gently manipulated to create a realistic pose.

## You will need

### Materials

- 24-gauge green wire
- 48-gauge green wire
- Spray adhesive
- A 5 x 8-in. sheet of translucent green paper
- An 8½ x 11-in. sheet of white decorative paper
- An 8½ x 11-in. sheet of white card
- Clear adhesive tape
- An 11 x 17-in. sheet of turquoise metallic cardstock
- Double-sided tape

### Tools

- Wire cutters or an old pair of scissors
- Scissors
- Craft knife
- Metal ruler
- Cutting mat
- Fine artist's paintbrush
- Large needle
- Bone folder (optional)

**1** Snip four 7½-inch lengths of 24-gauge wire for the wings with wire cutters or an old pair of scissors. Bend each length into a loop, overlapping the ends by ¾ inch. Twist a length of 48-gauge wire around the crossover of the thicker wire a few times to secure in place.

**2** Spray the wings with spray adhesive, and press them onto translucent green paper. Cut away the excess paper around the wings with a pair of scissors.

★★★ **Skill level**    🕐 **2 hours**    **Techniques:** *Scoring p. 11, Using spray adhesive p. 12, Strengthening paper p. 12*

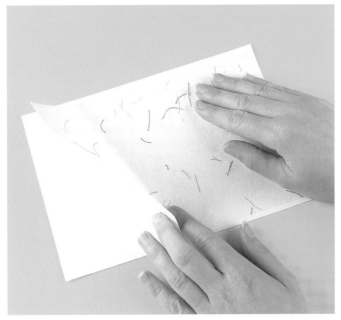

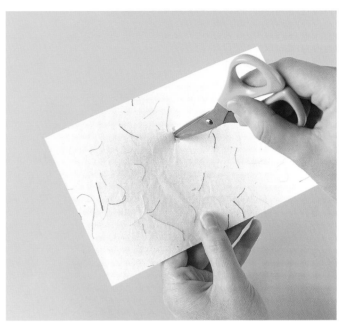

3  Apply a 5½ x 8¼-inch rectangle of white decorative paper to white cardstock with spray adhesive to stiffen it. Cut it down to a 4¾ x 7½-inch rectangle with a craft knife against a metal ruler as a guide. Work on a cutting mat.

4  With a craft knife, cut a ½-inch slit in the center that is 1½ inches down from the top of the stiffened paper. Push scissor blades through the slit to widen it enough for inserting the wires.

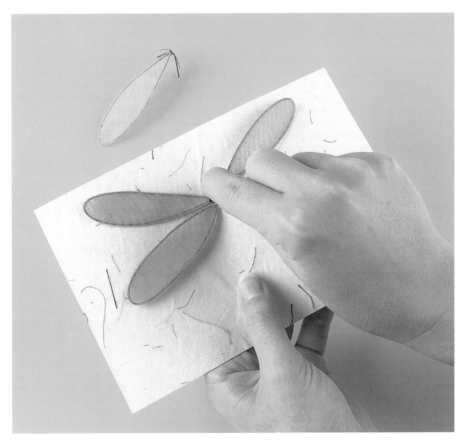

5  Bend the extending ends of the wing wires downwards at right angles, and insert them through the slit. Arrange the wings in pairs on each side of the slit. Bend back the wire ends under the stiffened paper, and splay them open. Stick pieces of clear adhesive tape over the wire ends to hold them in place.

## Helpful hint
The translucent paper used for the wings is a delicate, figured Japanese paper. Plain, colored tissue paper is an inexpensive but satisfactory alternative.

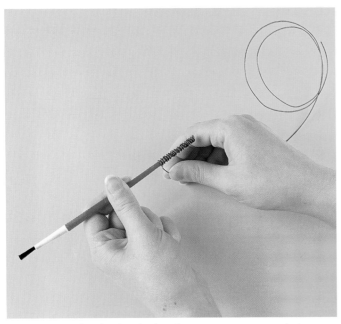

**6** To make the body, bind 24-gauge wire tightly around a fine artist's paintbrush starting at the top of the handle end. Continue binding until the coiled body is about 3 1/4 inches long. Slip the body off the paintbrush. Snip off the excess wire. Position the body over the wings.

**7** With a large needle, pierce a hole in the paper under the center of the body and another hole 3/4 inches below it. Thread 48-gauge wire up through one hole, then between a few coils of the body, and back through the other hole. Twist the ends together to hold the body to the paper.

**8** Cut a 9 x 12 1/2-inch rectangle of turquoise metallic cardstock. Using a bone folder or craft knife, score across the center parallel with the short edges. Fold the card in half along the scored line. Apply double-sided tape to the edges of the reverse side of the stiffened paper. Peel off the backing tapes and stick to the front of the card. Bend the body at a slight angle, and curve the center of the wings upward.

# Pierced and stitched seed head

**Making greetings cards and embroidery are the most popular of crafts. You can combine these mediums to make a pretty card using simple stitches on paper. The design is first pierced with a pin to provide a guide for the embroidery, which is worked with vibrant blue thread.**

Pearl cotton embroidery thread comes in lots of bright colors. Choose a shade that really stands out against your background paper.

## You will need

### Materials

- An 8½ x 11-in. sheet of pale orange mottled paper
- An 8½ x 11-in. sheet of cream cardstock
- Spray adhesive
- Tracing paper
- Masking tape
- Blue pearl cotton embroidery thread
- An 8½ x 11-in. sheet of silver cardstock

### Tools

- Scissors
- Soft pencil
- Cutting mat
- Glass-headed pin
- Embroidery needle
- Craft knife
- Metal ruler
- Bone folder (optional)

**1** To strengthen the background paper, glue together a 6 x 8-inch rectangle of pale orange mottled paper and cream cardstock using spray adhesive. Cut out a 4¼ x 7¼-inch rectangle with a pair of scissors. Shape one of the long sides.

**2** Trace the seed-head template on page 75 onto tracing paper with a soft pencil. Tape the tracing to the background paper with masking tape. Resting on a cutting mat, pierce a hole at each dot with a glass-headed pin. Remove the tracing.

★★★ **Skill level**    🕐 **4 hours**    **Techniques:** *Using templates p. 11, Using spray adhesive p. 12, Strengthening paper p. 12*

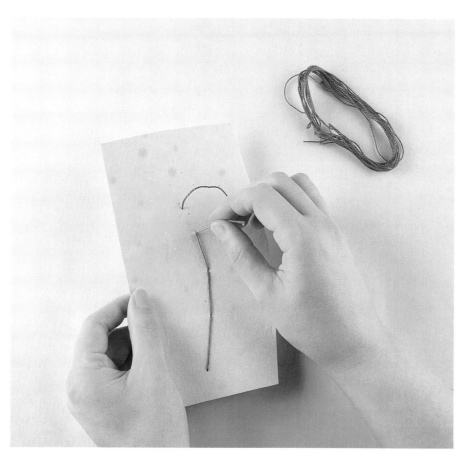

**3** Thread the needle with a length of embroidery thread. Knot the end. To work the stem in backstitch, bring the needle to the right side through the second hole from the bottom. Insert the needle through the lowest hole and up through the third hole, pulling the thread to lay smoothly on the paper. Continue to the top of the stem at the center of the seed-head.

**4** Now work the seed head in straight stitches, radiating out from the top of the stem.

**5** Place the background paper on the cutting mat. With the pin, pierce four holes around the end of each straight stitch for the seeds, which will be worked in French knots.

**6** Knot the thread end and bring it through a pierced hole to the right side. Twist the thread twice around the needle and then insert the needle back through the hole and pull the thread tight. Repeat on all the holes.

**7** Cut a 8¼ x 10½-inch rectangle of silver cardstock. Using a bone folder or craft knife, score across the center, parallel with the short edges. Fold the card in half along the scored line. Center the seed head to the front of the card, and adhere it with spray adhesive.

## Helpful hint
Choose a glass-headed pin instead of an ordinary dressmaking pin to pierce the design because it is much kinder to your fingers.

# Stenciled Asian screen

The chrysanthemum is often found decorating the beautiful screens and embroideries of the Far East. Re-create your own miniature Asian screen by stenciling a triptych card with trailing pink chrysanthemums. As a pretty finishing touch, the stenciled flowers are highlighted with gold relief paint.

*The chrysanthemum is the national flower of Japan and symbolizes purity and longevity.*

## You will need

### Materials

- Tracing paper
- Stencil board, 6½ x 10 in.
- Masking tape
- An 8½ x 11-in. sheet of gold and off-white marbled paper
- Mid-pink and deep pink acrylic paints
- Kitchen towel
- An 8½ x 11-in. sheet of purple cardstock
- Spray adhesive
- Gold relief paint

### Tools

- Soft pencil
- Scissors
- Cutting mat
- Craft knife
- Metal ruler
- ¾-in. and ½-in. stencil brushes
- Bone folder (optional)

**1** Trace the screen template on page 76 with a soft pencil onto tracing paper. Turn the paper over and re-draw the design. Tape the tracing, right side up, onto the stencil board with masking tape. Re-draw to transfer the design. Remove the tracing. Working on a cutting mat, cut out the stencil with a craft knife.

**2** Tape the stencil right side up on the marbled paper with masking tape. Pick up a little mid-pink paint on the ¾-inch stencil brush. Dab off the excess on a kitchen towel. Holding the brush upright, dab the paint through the stencils. Clean the brush.

★★★ **Skill level**    🕐 **4 hours**    **Techniques:** *Using templates p. 11, Using a craft knife p. 11, Using spray adhesive p. 12*

**3** Allow the paint to dry. Pick up a little deep pink paint on the ½-inch stencil brush, dabbing off the excess on a kitchen towel. Holding the brush upright, dab the paint in the center of each full flower and at the base of each quarter flower to shade them. Clean the brush and leave the paint to dry.

## Helpful hint
If you cannot find gold and cream marbled paper, create a similar effect by sponging gold paint randomly onto off-white paper with a natural sponge.

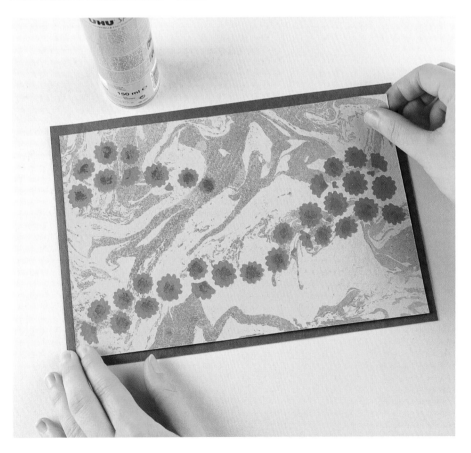

**4** Draw around the edges of the stencil on the marble paper, then cut out the rectangle. Cut a 7 x 10½-inch rectangle of purple card. Center the stenciled paper on the cardstock, adhering it with spray adhesive. Smooth the paper outwards.

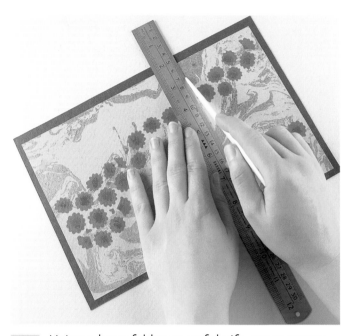

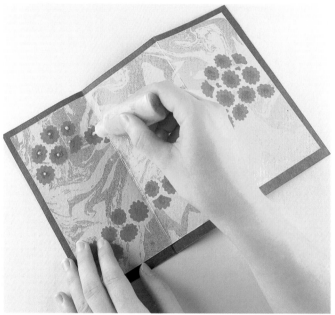

**5** Using a bone folder or craft knife, score across the screen 3½ inches in from both of the short sides of the cardstock. Fold the card accordian style along the two scored lines.

**6** Open the card out flat, and dot gold relief paint in the center of each full flower and at the base of each quarter flower. Leave it to dry, and then refold the card along the scored lines.

## Variation

### *Pink flowers*

This single fold greeting card has one-third of the stencil worked in white acrylic paint on colorful paper and applied to a folded pink card. The flowers are blushed with pale pink and highlighted with a bright pink relief paint.

# Glass-painted sun catcher

Glass paints applied to acetate give the effect of translucent stained glass. This exotic greeting card can also be given as a gift. The glass-painted design, inspired by Moorish tiles, is attached with a brass paper fastener and can be removed to suspend by a window where it will catch the sunlight.

Glass paints are easy to apply. The color is flooded into the reservoirs that have been created with glass painting outliner.

## You will need

### Materials
- Tracing paper
- Clear acetate
- Masking tape
- Gold glass-painting outliner
- White paper
- Scissors
- Pale blue, green, and deep blue glass paints
- An 11 x 17-in. sheet of white cardstock
- Brass paper fastener

### Tools
- Black pen
- Soft pencil
- Artist's paintbrush
- Cutting mat
- Craft knife
- Metal ruler
- Awl
- Bone folder (optional)

**1** Trace the card front on page 77 onto tracing paper with a black pen. Re-draw the peaks along the upper edge on the reverse side using a soft pencil. Tape the acetate over the tracing paper with masking tape. Trace the design onto the acetate with gold glass-painting outliner. Let it dry.

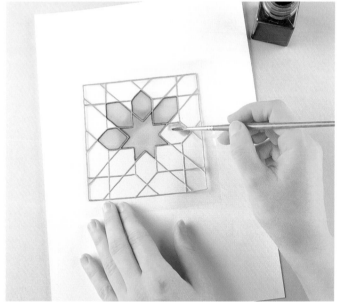

**2** Rest the acetate on white paper so that the painted areas will show clearly. Paint the central star areas pale blue. For each reservoir, load an artist's paintbrush with paint and place it in the center of the reservoir to fill the area with color. Brush the paint into the corners and up to the outliner.

★★★ **Skill level**    🕐 **4 hours**    **Techniques:** *Using templates p. 11, Using a craft knife p. 11, Scoring p. 11, Folding p. 12*

**3** Paint the small triangles surrounding the star green and the border deep blue. Let the paints dry overnight.

## Helpful hint
If you have not painted up to the outliner in all places, do not apply more paint or it will create an unattractive line of color. Instead, thicken the line with more outliner.

**4** Cut out the sun catcher. Working on a cutting mat, pierce a hole at the dot (refer to the tracing) with an awl. This is where the brass paper fastener will be positioned.

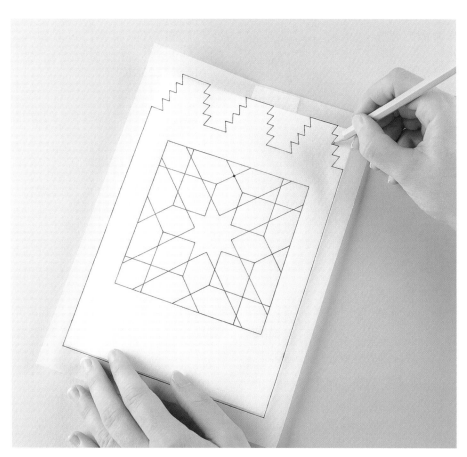

**5** Cut an 8 ½ x 12-inch rectangle of white cardstock. Using a bone folder or craft knife, score across the center of the card, parallel with the short edges. Fold the card in half along the scored line. Tape the tracing to the front of the card with masking tape. Redraw the upper edge to transfer the peaks. Also transfer the dot. Remove the tracing.

**6** Working on a cutting mat, cut out the peaks through both thicknesses of the cardstock using a craft knife. Open the card out flat. Working on the cutting mat, pierce a hole at the dot with an awl.

**7** Insert a brass paper fastener through the hole on the sun catcher, then through the hole on the card front. Splay open the prongs inside the card to secure the sun catcher in place.

# Painted-silk paisley series

It is sometimes useful to produce a series of greeting cards—for invitations, announcements, or holiday cards, for example. These painted-silk cards look very special but they are actually quick to produce in multiples at one time. For a quirky touch, the designs are applied to triangular cards—a great way to use up scraps of colored cardstock.

Apply white paper behind the silk if the motif is to be applied to colored cardstock. This prevents the cardstock showing through the fine fabric.

## You will need

### Materials

- 12-in. square of white medium-weight silk
- Tracing paper
- Masking tape
- Gold silk outliner (gutta)
- Blue, green, purple, and deep yellow silk paints
- 2 sheets of white tissue paper
- White paper
- Spray adhesive
- A 8½ x 11-in. sheets of colored card

### Tools

- Iron
- Soft pencil
- Scissors
- 12-in. silk frame
- 3-point silk pins
- Artist's paintbrush
- Cutting mat
- Craft knife
- Metal ruler
- Bone folder (optional)

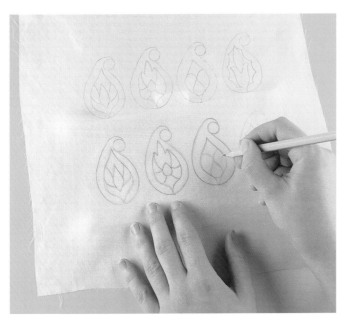

**1** Press the silk. Trace the paisley templates on page 77 onto tracing paper. Tape the silk on top with masking tape and trace a row of paisley motifs with a soft pencil. Remove the tracing. Use it again to trace another row of motifs below the first one.

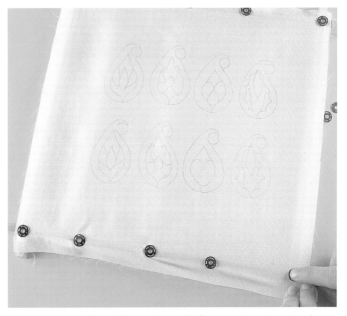

**2** Center the silk on the silk frame. Starting in the middle of one edge, pin the silk smoothly to the frame with 3-point silk pins. Repeat on the opposite edge of the frame and on the other two edges, smoothing the silk outwards toward the corners so that it lays flat and taut.

★★★ **Skill level**   🕐 **4 hours**   **Techniques:** *Using templates p. 11, Using a craft knife p. 11, Using spray adhesive p. 12*

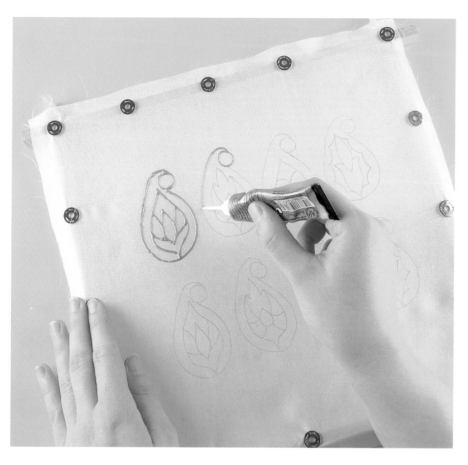

**3** Re-draw the rows of paisley motifs on the silk with gold silk outliner (gutta). Let it dry.

### Helpful hint

Before painting, check to see if any outliner (gutta) lines do not join up or are very thin. If this is the case, go over them again to fill any gaps so the paint cannot seep into the other sections.

**4** Dip the paintbrush into one of the silk paints. Press the brush onto the center of one of the areas, and allow the paint to flow up to the outline. Paint all of the paisley motifs, cleaning the paintbrush with water when changing colors. Set aside to dry.

**5** Using an iron, press the silk between two layers of white tissue paper to fix the paints. Roughly cut out the two rows of paisley motifs. Affix the rows to white paper with spray adhesive, smoothing the silk outward to eliminate air bubbles. Cut out each motif with a pair of scissors.

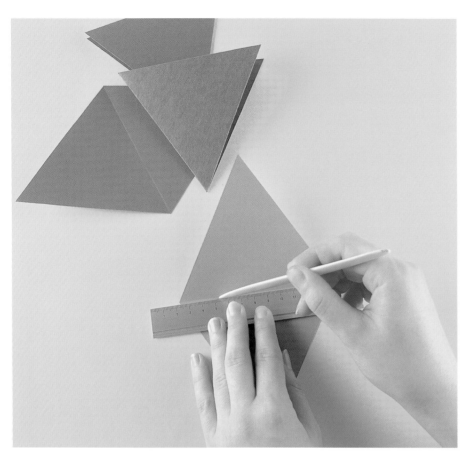

6 Trace the triangle template on page 77 onto tracing paper with a soft pencil. Turn the tracing paper over, and re-draw the triangle on the reverse side. Tape the tracing paper right side up onto one of the colored cards. Re-draw the triangle to transfer it. Repeat to draw eight triangles on the various colors. Working on a cutting mat and using a metal ruler, cut out the triangles with a craft knife. Score across the center of the triangle using a bone folder or craft knife.

7 Fold the card in half along the scored line. Mount a paisley motif to the front of each triangle with spray adhesive.

# Templates

*Templates shown are not full size. Photocopy them at 118% to correct the size for the projects.*

← **Embossed baby booties**
(pages 34–37)

← **Embossed baby booties**
(pages 34–37)

Roof

Roof tab position

House tab

Roof tab

Birdhouse

↑ **3-D birdhouse (pages 14–17)**

↑ **3-D birdhouse (pages 14–17)**

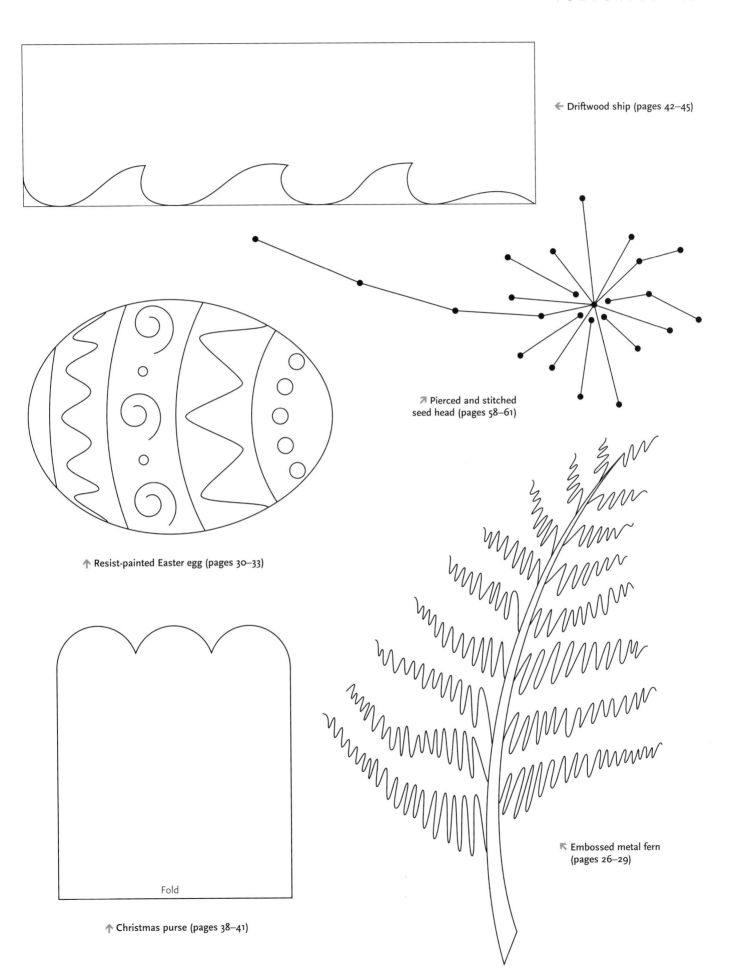

← Driftwood ship (pages 42–45)

↗ Pierced and stitched
seed head (pages 58–61)

↑ Resist-painted Easter egg (pages 30–33)

↖ Embossed metal fern
(pages 26–29)

Fold

↑ Christmas purse (pages 38–41)

*Templates shown are not full size. Photocopy them at 118% to correct the size for the projects.*

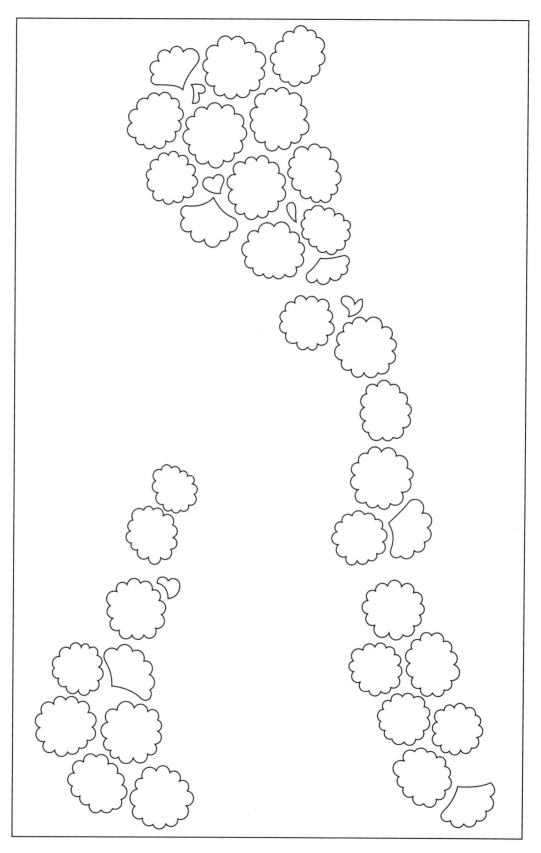

↑ Stenciled Asian screen (pages 62–65)

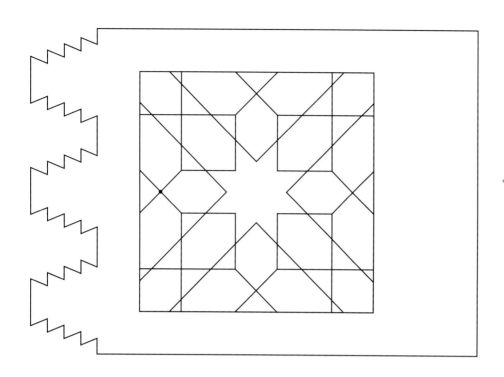

← Glass-painted sun catcher
(pages 66–69)

↙ Painted-silk paisley series
(pages 70–73)

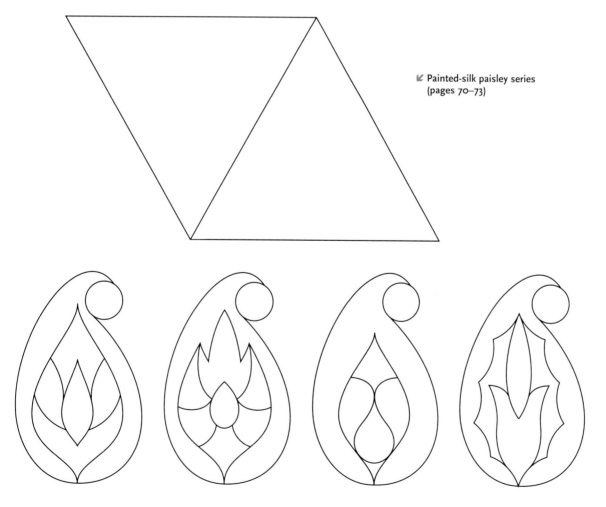

↑ Painted-silk paisley series (pages 70–73)

# Suppliers

## USA

**AccuCut**
1035 E. Dodge St.
Fremont, NE 68025
(800) 288-1670
www.accucut.com

**Arnold Grummer's**
830 N. 109th, Suite 1
Wauwatosa. WI 53226
(800) 453-1485
www.arnoldgrummer.com

**Autumn Leaves**
15821 Ventura Blvd., Suite 565
Encino, CA 91436
(800) 588-6707
www.autumnleaves.com

**Colorbok**
2716 Baker Rd.
Dexter, MI 48130
(734) 426-5300
www.colorbok.com

**Crane and Company**
30 South St.
Dalton, MA 01226
(800) 268-2281
www.crane.com

**Deluxe Cuts**
P.O. Box 8283
Mesa, AZ 85214
(480) 497-9005
www.deluxecuts.com

**Delta**
2550 Pellissier Place
Whittier, CA 90601
(800) 423-4135
www.deltacrafts.com

**Destination Stickers and Stamps**
P.O. Box 15027
Fort Wayne, IN 46885
(260) 482-4047
www.journeystamps.com

**Ellison Craft and Design**
25862 Commercentre Dr.
Lake Forest, CA 92630
(949) 598-8822
www.ellison.com

**Elmer's Products**
180 E. Broad St.
Columbus, OH 43215
(614) 225-4000
www.elmers.com

**Fiskars**
7811 W. Stewart Ave.
Wausau, WI 54401
(800) 500-4849
www.fiskars.com

**Grumbacher**
(800) 323-0749
(800) 668-4575 in Canada
www.sanford.com

**Heart of the Home Stencils**
17516 Chesterfield
Airport Road, Cabin B
Chesterfield, MO 63005
(888) 519-1768
www.stencils4u.com

**Inkadinkado**
61 Holton St.
Woburn, MA 01801
(800) 888-4652
www.inkadinkado.com

**Loew-Cornell**
563 Chestnut Ave.
Teanuck, NJ 07666
(201) 836-8110
www.loew-cornell.com

**Musgrave Pencil Company**
P.O. Box 290
Shelbyville, TN 37162
(931) 684-3611
www.pencils.net

**National Cardstock**
132 Perry Hwy., Bldg. 2
Harmony PA 16037
(724) 452-7120

**Paper Adventures**
90 S. Fifth St.
Milwaukee, WI 04607
(800) 876-2273
www.paperadventures.com

**The Paper Co.**
510 Ryerson Rd.
Lincoln Park, NJ 07035
(800) 525-3196
www.anwcrestwood.com

**Paper House Productions**
(800) 255-7316
www.paperproductions.com

**Paper Patch**
P.O. Box 47098
Celebration, FL 34747
(407) 566-0720

**Paperfever Inc.**
711 Goldenrod Ave.
Corona del Mar, CA 92625
(949) 70-9663
www.paperfever.com

**Pazzles**
3633 Green Lane
Kuna, ID 83634
www.pazzles.com

**The Pencil Grip**
P.O. Box 670 96
Los Angeles, CA 90067
(310) 315-3545
www.thepencilgrip.com

**Plaid Industries**
P.O. Box 7600
Norcross, GA 30091
(800) 842-4197
www.plaidonline.com

**Prairie Craft Co.**
P.O. Box 209
Florissant, CO 90816
(800) 779-0615
www.prairiecraft.com

**Sizzix.com**
25862 Commercentre Dr.
Lake Forest, CA 92630
(877) 355-4766
www.sizzix.com

**Some Assembly Required**
PMB 14
3703 S. Edmund St.
Seattle, WA 98118
www.some-assembly-required.com

**Stensource International**
(800) 642-9293
www.stensource.com

## CANADA

**Aw Cute Stickers N'Stuff**
3581 Dunbarton Rd.
Westbank, BC V4T 1J3
(250) 768-4346
www.awcute.com

**Beary Patch**
Box 188
Cardston, Alberta T04 1E0
www.bearypatchinc.com

**Bisous**
89-720 Avonwick Ave.
Mississauga, ON L5R 4C6
(905) 502-7209
www.bisous.biz

**Heart & Home**
530 Westney Rd. S. 9
Ajax, ON L1S 6W3
(905) 686-9031
www.heartandhome.com

**Magenta**
2275 Bombardier
Sainte-Julie, Quebec J3E 2Jp
(450) 922-5253
www.magentastyle.com

**Metropolis Paper Int. Inc.**
70 Clayson Rd.
Toronto, ON M9M 2G7
(416) 740-4345
www.evergreen-metropolis.com

**Paper Tole Designs**
1180 Kerrisdale Blvd. 1
New Market, ON L3Y 7V1
(905) 853-4488
www.papertoledesigns.com

## ASSOCIATIONS

## USA

**American Craft Council**
21 S. Eltings Corner Rd.
Highland, NY 12528
(800) 836-3470
www.craftcouncil.org

**Arts and Crafts Association of America**
4888 Cannon Woods Ct.
Belmont, MI 49306
(616) 874-1721
www.artsandcraftsassoc.com

**Association of Crafts & Creative Industries**
1100-H Brandywine Blvd.
P.O. Box 3388
Zanesville, OH 43702
(740) 452-4541
www.accicrafts.org

**Hobby Industry Association**
319 E. 54th St.
Elmwood Park, NJ 07407
(201) 794-1133
www.hobby.org

**National Craft Association**
1945 E. Ridge Rd., Suite 5178
Rochester, NY 14622
(800) 715-9594

## CANADA

**Canada Craft and Hobby Association**
24 1410-40 Ave,. N.E.
Calgary, AL T2E 6L1
(403) 291-0559

**Canadian Carfts Federation**
c/o Ontario Crafts Council
Designers Walk
170 Bedford Rd., Suite 300
Toronto, ON M5R 2K9
(416) 408-2294
www.canadiancraftsfederation.ca

# Index